Martin Jacoby

Descriptions of the new species of phytophagous Coleoptera

Martin Jacoby

Descriptions of the new species of phytophagous Coleoptera

ISBN/EAN: 9783741130533

Manufactured in Europe, USA, Canada, Australia, Japa

Cover: Foto ©Thomas Meinert / pixelio.de

Manufactured and distributed by brebook publishing software (www.brebook.com)

Martin Jacoby

Descriptions of the new species of phytophagous Coleoptera

Entomologische Zeitung

herausgegeben von dem

entomologischen Vereine

zu Stettin.

Redaction: Dr. **Heinrich Dohrn,** Vorsitzender.

In Commission bei der Buchhandlung R. Friedländer & Sohn in Berlin.

No. 10–12. 60. Jahrgang. IV. Heft 1899.

Descriptions of the New Species of Phytophagous Coleoptera obtained by Dr. Dohrn in Sumatra

by

Martin Jacoby.

(with plate.)

Dr. H. Dohrn has kindly submitted to me for determination and description, the collection of Phytophaga obtained by him at the East coast of Sumatra in the province of Deli; the exact localities where the specimens were obtained together with other particulars, have been given by Dr. Dohrn, in the Stettiner Zeitung for 1898 as a preface to the descriptions by Mr. Krüger, of the Neuroptera obtained at the same localities. In regard to the Phytophaga a very large number of species were collected by Dr. Dohrn, many of which are new and interesting. Although there is no doubt that the great island of Sumatra is at present very imperfectly explored in regard to its entomological treasures, yet we begin to get gradually a pretty fair idea of its fauna. Wallace, D'Alberti, Beccari, many Dutch entomologists and others have visited the island and Baly, Duvivier and myself have worked out the Phytophagous Coleoptera from the material obtained by these explorers: in spite of this, nearly 50 new species are here described and many remain at present undetermined for want of more material. Besides these new species, Dr. Dohrn's collection contains very many previously described forms which I have not thought it necessary again to enumerate.

Sumatra seems certainly to have more species in common with India than with any other parts in this group of Coleoptera as well as in others and justifies its being included in the Indo-Malayan region. Of former publications on Sumatran Phytophaga the following may be mentioned:

Baly. Phytophaga Malayana in Transactions Entom. Soc. London. 1867.

Jacoby. Midden-Sumatra. Leyden 1886.

- Descriptions of new Genera and Species of Phytophagous Coleoptera from the Indo-Malayan and Austro-Malayan subregions in Annali del Muse Civico di Genova 1886. Serie 2. Vol. IV.
- Notes from the Leyden Museum 1887.
- Stettiner Entomol. Zeitung 1895.
- Annali del Museo Civico di Storia naturale di Genova 1896.

Besides these publications numerous other species from Sumatra have been described by Lefèvre, Duvivier, Allard and myself in different entomological Journals. A few species from the island of Sumba were likewise obtained by Dr. Dohrn and are described here.

Crioceridae.

Lema sumbaensis sp. n.

Fulvous, the antennae (the basal joints excepted), black, thorax slightly longer than broad, nearly impunctate, elytra metallic blue, strongly punctate-striate anteriorly, more finely so posteriorly, the ninth row entire.

Length 6 mill.

Stett. entomol. Zeit. 1899.

Head not much constricted behind the eyes, impunctate, fulvous as well as the labrum, antennae extending slightly below the base of the elytra, black, the basal two joints fulvous, the second joint moniliform, the third and fourth joints equal, the terminal three joints shorter than the preceding ones; thorax very slightly longer than broad, the sides not much constricted, the basal sulcus shallow, the disc with some extremely fine punctures at the middle and anteriorly, the anterior angles rounded, scutellum small, dark fulvous, its apex truncate, elytra with a shallow depression below the base, metallic blue, regularly and rather strongly punctate-striate anteriorly, the punctures gradually decreasing in size towards the apex, where they are very closely placed, almost forming striae, the interstices at the same place convex, impunctate; below sparingly pubescent, fulvous as well as the legs, the latter more closely covered with yellowish pubescence.

Hab. Sumba.

Similar in its general coloration to many other Eastern *Lema's* but differing in the shape of the thorax and the black antennae, fulvous legs etc.

Lema verrucosa sp. n. (Fig. 1).

Fulvous, the antennae (the apical joints excepted) black; thorax impunctate, with a central piceous stripe; elytra black, foveolate-punctate, the interstices strongly elevate and reticulate.

Length 6 mill.

Head elongate, fulvous, eyes deeply notched, antennae extending below the middle of the elytra, black, the terminal two or three joints fulvous, third joint twice the length of the second one; thorax scarcely longer than broad, the anterior portion subcylindrical, the angles rounded, the middle deeply constricted, the basal sulcus deep and ending in the lateral constriction, the surface impunctate, the disc with a narrow piceous stripe, more or less distinct; scutellum black, its apex truncate;

elytra wider at the base than the thorax, without basal depression, black, shining, the basal margin sometimes stained with fulvous, the surface deeply foveolate, the interstices everywhere strongly convex and partly confluent and forming short costae near the apex; below and the legs fulvous, clothed with short yellow pubescence; claws piceous.

Closely allied to *L. variolosa* Baly but the antennae of different colour, the elytra without basal depression and with the interstices raised throughout the surface, the legs entirely fulvous; three specimens from Soekaranda.

Temnaspis Dohrni sp. n. (Fig. 3).

Black, pubescent, above rufous, antennae paler, head finely, thorax srongly and closely punctured, elytra finely punctured, pubescent, each with a black central spot or band near the suture.

Mas. Posterior femora with a strong spine, metasternum bituberculate.

Length 9—11 mill.

Head fulvous, very closely and finely punctured with a central fovea at the vertex, sparingly clothed with yellow pubescence, antennae flavous, the lower four joints darker and shining, the others opaque, clothed with yellow pubescence, the joints transversely subquadrate; thorax scarcely twice as broad as long, narrowed anteriorly, the sides slightly rounded, the disc raised at each side, the raised portion divided by central and lateral depression, closely and strongly punctured and clothed with flavous hairs, scutellum broad, its apex truncate; elytra much wider at the base than the thorax, rather strongly depressed near the middle, finely and rather closely punctured in irregular rows, the interstices furnished with single long yellow pubescence, a black spot of variable size and sometimes in shape of a short transverse band extends across the suture at the middle, the underside and the legs black, clothed with silvery white pubescence, the anterior femora flavous, the posterior femora very robust, armed at their outer edge with a strong spur or spine in the male, the metasternum in the same sex raised at each side into a strong conical protuberance.

Four specimens of this species were obtained by Dr. Dohrn at Soekaranda: they differ from any of their allies in the system of coloration.

Temnaspis nigricollis sp. n. (Fig. 2).

Black, the labrum, palpi, antennae and the tarsi flavous; the head closely, the thorax finely and sparingly punctured and pubescent; elytra red, finely punctured, sides of the breast and abdomen, flavous.

Mas. Posterior femora with a stout spine, metasternum bituberculate.

Length 10 mill.

Head elongate, strongly constricted behind the eyes, finely and closely punctured at the vertex, the latter with a fovea, two others placed near the eyes, these organs very large and prominent, labrum and palpi flavous, antennae entirely flavous, the lower four joints shining, the rest opaque, subquadrately widened; thorax one half broader than long, narrowed anteriorly, the posterior angles prominent and oblique, the disc with a transverse groove near the anterior margin, deeply impressed at the sides, rest of the surface rather convex, with an oblique depression at the base at each side, black, shining, sparingly punctured and pubescent, the hairs of black colour, scutellum fulvous; elytra of a bright red colour, clothed with fulvous pubescence, transversely depressed below the base, finely punctured: below black, the sides more or less flavous, legs black, the tibiae more or less fulvous at their inner side, the tarsi flavous, the posterior femora in the male with a stout tooth near the apex, clothed like the rest of the legs with long yellowish and black hairs.

Distinguished by the black head and thorax and the bright red elytra.

From Soekaranda and Liangagas.

Gynandrophthalma occipitalis sp. n.

Fulvous, the vertex of the head, the antennae, the breast and the legs more or less black, thorax impunctate, elytra extremely finely punctured, black, shining.

Var. The underside and the femora fulvous.

Length 5 mill.

Head impunctate, fulvous, the vertex more or less black, shining, clypeus not separated from the face, impunctate, its anterior edge but feebly emarginate, eyes large, entire, antennae black, the lower three joints fulvous, the fourth and following joints very broadly flattened and dilated, pubescent, extending beyond the base of the thorax, the latter transverse, more than twice as broad as long, the sides nearly straight, the angles obtusely rounded, the surface entirely impunctate, reddish-fulvous, very shining, scutellum broad, its apex pointed, fulvous, elytra very shining, black, with rows of very minute punctures, closely placed; below clothed with fine yellow pubescence, the breast and legs blackish or fulvous, the first joint of the posterior tarsi as long as the following two joints together.

Soekaranda.

Aspidolopha imperialis Baly var. (Fig. 4).

The single specimen of this species which is contained in this collection, belongs to a variety in which the elytral bands are united and occupy the entire disc.

Aspidolopha capitata sp. n.

Pale fulvous, densely pubescent below, antennae (the basal joints excepted) black, vertex of the head dark blue, thorax nearly impunctate, elytra very closely and finely punctured.

Length 8 mill.

Of subcylindrical shape, the vertex of the head finely rugose, dark blue, this colour divided from the fulvous portion by a straight line, clypeus separated from the face by a triangular, closely punctured depression, its anterior edge concave, more or less piceous as well as the labrum, the antennae extending to the base of the thorax, black, the lower four joints fulvous, terminal joints strongly triangularly widened, thorax at least twice as broad as long, the sides slightly rounded, obliquely narrowed towards the apex, the median lobe broad, distinct, the surface impunctate, with the exception of a few fine punctures near the margins; scutellum broad, fulvous, its apex truncate; elytra parallel, strongly lobed below the shoulders, very closely and finely punctured, the apex nearly impunctate, the underside densely clothed with silky yellow pubescence; legs long and robust, the first joint of the posterior tarsi as long as the following two joints together.

Easily separated from its allies by the uniform fulvous coloration and the blue vertex of the head. Three specimens from Soekaranda.

Bucharis laevicollis sp. n.

Black, the basal joints of the antennae, the lower portion of the face and the legs fulvous, thorax impunctate, elytra with finely punctured striae, the base deeply punctured.

Length 2 mill.

Upper portion of the head entirely occupied by the eyes, which meet at the top, the clypeus fulvous, labrum piceous, antennae short, extending to the base of the thorax only, the terminal joints short and thickened, black, the lower five joints fulvous; thorax more than twice as broad as long, nearly subcylindrical, the sides strongly deflexed, the lateral margins nearly straight, strongly narrowed anteriorly, the anterior margin preceded by a transverse groove, the posterior one accompanied by a row of deep punctures, the rest of the surface entirely impunctate, the sides with a narrow oblique groove, the base of the posterior margin pointed at the middle, fitting into the base of the scutellum, the latter lanceolate, narrow, elytra subcylindrical, black, very shining, evenly and strongly striate-punctate, the punctures of elongate shape, those at the base deep and large, the interstices impunctate costate at the sides; below black, the legs fulvous; prosternum much broader than long.

Hab. Liangagas.

In the constraction of the eyes which occupy the entire sides and top of the head, this species agrees with *B. oculatus* Jac. likewise inhabiting Sumatra, but the strongly transverse and entirely impunctate thorax at once separate *B. laevicollis* from this and the other species of the genus. Three specimens.

Oomorphus caeruleus sp. n.

Below black, above dark blue, thorax finely and subremotely punctured, elytra more strongly punctured in closely approached, semiregular rows; prosternum strongly narrowed posteriorly.

Length 4 mill.

Of strongly convex and posteriorly narrowed shape, the head flat, impunctate, bluish, the clypeus separated from the face by an obsolete semicircular depression, antennae very short, black, the second joint short and stout, the intermediate ones slender, the apical joints strongly widened, thorax transverse, narrowed anteriorly, the sides nearly straight, oblique, the basal margin sinuate at the sides, its median lobe semiacute, the surface very finely but not closely punctured; scutellum very small; elytra strongly narrowed posteriorly, very convex, the apex rounded, the disc more strongly punctured than the thorax, the punctures arranged in rather closely approached, semiregular rows; below and the legs bluish-black, the prosternum much longer than broad, strongly narrowed posteriorly, the claws simple.

Closely allied to *O. sumatrana* Jac. but of blue not black colour, the elytra more strongly, closely and less regularly punctured.

From Soekaranda.

Eumolpidae.

Nodina fulvicollis sp. n.

Dark fulvous or piceous below, the head, antennae and thorax fulvous, the latter, remotely and strongly punctured, elytra pointed posteriorly, black, strongly subgeminate punctate-striate.

Length 3 mill.

Head with a few fine punctures, fulvous, the middle with a longitudinal groove, clypeus separated from the face, subquadrate, impunctate, antennae fulvous (the last joints wanting) third and the following two joints elongate; thorax more than twice as broad as long, the sides feebly rounded, strongly deflexed, the surface remotely and rather strongly punctured, fulvous, the spaces near the margins nearly impunctate, scutellum piceous, elytra very convex, strongly pointed at the apex, the shoulders prominent, the punctures strong and arranged in eight, not very regular double rows, the outer two interstices more or less costate towards the apex, the latter obscure fulvous; below and the legs dark fulvous, stained with piceous, the posterior femora entirely of the latter colour.

At once distinguished from any other species of the genus by the fulvous head and thorax; the black colour of the elytra gradually changes to fulvous at the extreme apex. Two specimens from Soekaranda.

Nodostoma Dohrni sp. n.

Fulvous, the eighth and ninth joint of the antennae black, two apical ones white, thorax impunctate with a central black spot, elytra with deep basal depression, nearly impunctate, the sutural and lateral margins and a spot within the depression, black, knees and tarsi piceous, anterior femora strongly dentate.

Length 6 mill.

Head impunctate, fulvous, clypeus wedgeshaped, separated from the face by deep lateral grooves, the sides of which are strongly raised at the base of the antennae, its surface impunctate, the anterior edge deeply concave, mandibles black, antennae long and slender, fulvous, the eighth and ninth joints black, the terminal two joints whitish, the fourth and the following joints distinctly longer than the third; thorax not more than one half broader than long, the sides rounded, the angles prominent, the disc with a transverve groove in front of the anterior margin, entirely impunctate, fulvous, the middle with a black lozenge-shape spot, scutellum fulvous; elytra deeply depressed below the base, the basal portion raised, deeply punctured within the depression only and in front of the shoulders, the rest of the surface nearly impunctate, fulvous, the sutural and lateral margins narrowly black, the disc with an elongate or more transverse shaped black spot placed within the basal depression; underside and legs fulvous, the latter elongate, the anterior femora with a stout tooth, the posterior ones less strongly toothed, the knees and the tarsi more or less black or piceous.

Soekarandа.

Almost entirely similar in coloration as *N. apicicorne* Lefèv. excepting the antennae which have the 4th to the 9th joint black in the latter species; in the same insect the vertex of the head is rugose-punctate and the thorax strongly punctured, both parts in the present species are entirely free from punctures. *N. nigromaculatum* Lefèv. has differently coloured antennae and a punctured thorax, also a short elytral costa at the shoulders.

Aulexis longicornis sp. n.

Testaceous, closely pubescent, antennae nearly as long as the body in the male, the head and thorax obscure piceous or fulvous, closely punctured, elytra punctured like the thorax, clothed with silvery grey pubescence.

Length 5 mill.

Head very finely punctured at the vertex, the epistome strongly but remotely punctate, the eyes very large, antennae extending nearly to the apex of the elytra, pale testaceous, the second and third joints nearly equal, both short, the others elongate, thorax with deep lateral sulci, the sides threedentate, the anterior portion punctured like the head, the basal part, closely and strongly punctate, the surface pubescent like the elytra, the latter of paler colour, punctured like the base of the thorax, punctuation nearly obsolete near the apex, the underside of rather darker colour than the upper surface, finely and sparingly pubescent.

Soekaranda and Liangagas.

This *Aulexis* is one of the smaller species, distinguished by the long antennae, the very finely punctured head and anterior portion of the thorax in connection with its coloration the elytra being of paler colour than the other parts. Whether this species is identical with *A. pallida* Lefèv. likewise from Sumatra I am not able to say, as the description is not detailed enough: the general colour of the insect is described as pale fulvous; no mention is made of the different punctuation at the basal portion of the thorax or its darker colour and the description applies nearly equally to any species of the genus since mainly generic characters are given. Lefèvre's species moreover is four millim. in length. The specimens which I look upon as females of the present insect have much shorter antennae, the latter only extending below the base of the elytra, but other differences I am not able to find.

Aulexis elongata Jac.

Specimens from Liangagas and Soekaranda agree well with the typical form described by me from Si-Rambé, in Sumatra: the colour of the antennae which is black, excepting the three or four basal joints, well distinguish this insect, but the legs are subject to variation in this respect, in most case however they are flavous, with the tarsi more or less piceous.

Aulexis Wallacei Baly.

There are specimens from Soekaranda and Liangagas before me which vary greatly in size but not in any essential characters warranting a specific separation, the head and thorax in all is blackish, but in three specimens (females) the same parts are fulvous, although the size and sculpture agrees with the type; all the species of this genus are probably much subject to variation and much material is required to satisfactory separate them.

Tricliona fulvifrons sp. n.

Black, the head, the basal joints of the antennae, the abdomen and the legs fulvous; thorax very finely punctured, elytra punctate-striate at the base only, black, the apex flavous.

Length 5 mill.

Head impunctate, fulvous, clypeus not separated from the face, eyes very large, their diameter broader than the space dividing them, antennae extending to the middle of the elytra, filiform, black, the lower four joints fulvous, third and fourth joints equal; thorax twice as broad as long, the sides rounded, the angles distinct, the surface finely punctured, the spaces in front of the lateral margins impunctate, elytra wider at the base than the thorax, distinctly depressed below the base, strongly punctate-striate at the latter place, the punctures gradually disappearing below the middle, black, the apex more or less flavous, thorax below and the breast black, the abdomen and the legs fulvous, the anterior femora dilated into a strong triangular tooth, the other femora with a small tooth.

Soekaranda.

Of shining black colour, easily distinguished by the fulvous head and the flavous apex of the elytra.

Colaspoides fulvitarsis sp. n.

Obscure dark blue below, above purplish-black, the basal joints of the antennae and the tarsi fulvous, head closely, thorax remotely punctured, elytra finely punctate-striate, transversely depressed below the base, legs unarmed.

Var. The head, underside and the legs fulvous.

Length 5—5½ mill.

Of convex, oblong shape, nearly black with a slight purplish tint, the head more distinctly blue, very finely and closely punctured, the clypeus more strongly punctured, the labrum fulvous, antennae rather short, the terminal joints strongly thickened, black, the lower eight joints more or less fulvous; thorax nearly three times broader than long, the sides rounded, narrowly margined, the surface widened at the middle, strongly convex, very finely and remotely punctured; elytra not wider at the base than the thorax, ovate convex, distinctly depressed below the base, finely punctured in rather closely approached regular rows, the punctures at the sides and within the depression stronger, the interstices smooth and impunctate, the space between the shoulders and the lateral margin raised and smooth; below and the legs bluish, the femora unarmed, the tarsi fulvous.

Soekaranda.

This *Colaspoides* differs in coloration from any of its Eastern congeners, the variety or aberration probably represents an immature specimen.

Cleoporus sumbaensis sp. n.

Fulvous, terminal joints of the antennae black, thorax finely and subremotely punctured, elytra greenish-aeneous, strongly punctate-striate.

Var. Thorax aeneous.

Length 4 mill.

Head fulvous with a slight aeneous gloss, finely and sparingly punctured, the eyes surrounded by a broad sulcus, clypeus separated by a transverse groove, transversely subquadrate, its anterior edge slightly emarginate at the middle, labrum fulvous, antennae not extending to the middle of the elytra, black the lower five joints fulvous, the third joint slightly longer than the fourth; thorax subcylindrical, one half broader than long, the sides straight, slightly oblique, the surface finely but not very closely punctured, scutellum piceous, elytra subcylindrical, aeneous, strongly and regularly punctate-striate, the striae at the sides abbreviated below the shoulders and before the apex, the interstices at the same places more or less costate, below and the legs fulvous, the anterior femora rather strongly dilated into a tooth, the others to a less degree so, the posterior four tibiae emarginate at the apex, the claws bifid, the anterior margin of the thoracic episternum convex; prosternum broad.

Hab. Sumba Island.

I cannot separate from this species specimens which have the vertex of the head as well as the entire thorax coloured like the elytra, there are no other structural differences.

Halticinae.

Aphthona flaveola sp. n.

Flavous, the antennae (the basal three joints excepted) black, thorax subquadrate, impunctate, elytra with a few microscopically fine punctures, tarsi stained with fuscous.

Length 3 mill.

Head impunctate, the vertex more or less piceous or dark fulvous, frontal tubercles transverse, clypeus with a central ridge, antennae extending to the middle of the elytra, rather robust, black, the lower three joints fulvous, second and third joints short, equal, fourth as long as the two preceding joints together; thorax scarcely one half broader than long, the sides nearly straight, the anterior angles slightly thickened, the surface impunctate, elytra rather convex, with a few scarcely perceptible punctures, below and the legs flavous, the tarsi slightly stained with fuscous.

Hab. Sumba.

This species resembles several European forms in its uniform flavous coloration, but the antennae are nearly black, the thorax has almost straight sides and is but little convex and the elytra are slightly widened at the apex.

Sebaethe depressa sp. n.

Oblong-ovate, depressed, pale fulvous or testaceous, the intermediate joints of the antennae black, thorax fulvous, impunctate, elytra distinctly and closely punctured, testaceous, a narrow transverse band at the base and a broader one behind the middle, black.

Length 4—5 mill.

Of flattened shape, the head impunctate, shining, frontal tubercles narrowly transverse, the clypeus perpendicularly deflexed, with an acute central ridge, antennae rather long and slender, the lower three and the terminal two joints, fulvous, the others black, basal joint elongate, the third joint one half longer than the second one, thorax strongly transverse, of equal width, the sides rounded, with a narrow reflexed margin, the angles acute, the surface impunctate, fulvous, elytra widened towards the middle, flattened, closely and finely, but distinctly punctured, the punctures nearly obsolete near the apex, the ground colour testaceous, the base with a narrow transverse black band, surrounding the shoulders, another broader band is placed below the middle and is widened at the sides, extending a little way upwards at the latter place, below and the legs testaceous or fulvous, the posterior femora strongly incrassate, abdomen finely pubescent.

Liangagas, Sinabong.

Allied to *S. 4-pustulata* Baly but of totally different shape, not convex but depressed, the antennae of different colour and the elytral bands not connected by a sutural black stripe.

Sphaeroderma semiregularis sp. n.

Below and the legs more or less piceous, above fulvous, antennae black, the lower two and the apical joint fulvous, thorax extremely closely and finely punctured, elytra finely punctured, the punctuation arranged in partly regular rows, the interstices more irregularly punctured.

Length 5 mill.

Head impunctate, the frontal elevations broad and obliquely shaped, the carina convex and strongly raised, terminal joint of the palpi robust, elongate and pointed, antennae extending beyond the base of the elytra, black, the basal two and the apical joint fulvous, the second and third joint equal, robust, short, the following joints widened, apical joint acute, thorax nearly three times broader than long, the sides obliquely narrowed towards the apex, the anterior angles thickened, the basal margin sinuate at each side near the scutellum, the entire surface very minutely and closely punctured, elytra slightly narrowed at the apex, the latter rounded, the surface more strongly punctured than the thorax, the punctures arranged in semi-regular rather distant rows which become obsolete near the apex, extra punctures are placed between the rows and some very fine punctures are also seen at the interstices when viewed under a strong lens, elytral epipleurae very broad and concave, below partly or entirely piceous, the legs nearly black, prosternum much broader than long, metasternum strongly punctured.

Soekaranda und Liangagas.

This species differs from *S. Rafflesi* Jac. in the shape of the frontal elevations of the head, which, although rather broad, are much narrower than in that species and obliquely shape, the antennae have the basal two joints fulvous only and the elytral punctuation is finer and more distantly placed and the underside and legs are not fulvous but piceous; *S. Modiglianii* Jac. another closely allied species from Sumatra, has likewise very broad and flattened frontal tubercles, the antennae extending to the middle of the elytra and their basal four joints fulvous, the thorax is still more transversely shaped, its anterior angles distinctly oblique and the elytral punctuation is close and strong.

Sphaeroderma nigromarginatum sp. n.

Fulvous, the apical joints of the antennae and the posterior legs black, thorax extremely finely and closely punctured, elytra more distinctly and rather closely punctate-striate, the sides from the base to the middle black.

Length 4—5 mill.

Head impunctate, the frontal tubercles nearly obsolete, broad, the carina not acutely raised, rather broad, antennae extending to the base of the elytra, black, the lower three joints fulvous, the third joint slightly longer than the second, the following joints thickened and closely pubescent, thorax more than twice as broad as long, scarcely narrowed in front, the sides nearly straight, the anterior angles obtuse, the surface microscopically punctured, elytra finely punctured in closely approached rows, the lateral margins from the base to below the middle black, below dark fulvous or piceous, the abdomen paler, the posterior legs black.

Sinabong.

Of this species I have two specimens before me, one obtained by Dr. Dohrn which is smaller and has the sides of the thorax black as well as those of the elytra, and another, contained in my collection, likewise from Sumatra in which the thorax is entirely fulvous, but this specimen does not differ in any other way from the smaller one and is no doubt only a variety: I know of no other *Sphaeroderma* from this region, similarly marked.

Sphaeroderma seminigrum sp. n.

Dark fulvous below, the head, antennae (the basal joints excepted) and the thorax black, elytra fulvous, extremely finely punctured in semi-regular rows, legs black.

Length 3 mill.

Head impunctate, black, the frontal tubercles very small, labrum flavous, eyes very large, antennae short and robust, black, the lower three joints flavous, the second and third joints equal, the terminal joints strongly thickened; thorax of usual transverse shape, the sides nearly straight, the surface extremely minutely and rather closely punctured, the median lobe produced and rounded, scutellum small, fulvous, elytra more strongly punctured, in closely approached, semiregular rows; below fulvous, the legs black, the tarsi more or less fulvous again.

Soekaranda and Liangagas.

A small species and resembling several others from the East in many structural details, but differing in the black head and thorax in connection with the large eyes and the black legs; in one specimen the lateral margin of the elytra is partly black also.

Hyphasis abdominalis sp. n.

Black, the thorax flavous, impunctate, elytra extremely minutely punctured anteriorly, black, abdomen more or less flavous.

Length 5 mill.

Of elongate shape, the head impunctate, black, very shining, deeply transversely grooved between the eyes, the latter very large, the frontal elevations strongly raised, trigonate, contiguous the clypeus deflexed, the antennae extending beyond the middle of the elytra, black, the second joint slightly shorter than the third, the following joints nearly equal, longer than the third joint; thorax twice as broad as long, the sides moderately rounded, with a narrow margin, the anterior angles thickened and slightly produced, the surface convex, impunctate, flavous, scutellum black; elytra scarcely perceptibly punctured at the anterior portion only, the rest impunctate, black, shining, with a very narrow reflexed, obscure fulvous margin, their epipleurae very broad and concave, below black, the posterior femora strongly incrassate, the first joint of the posterior tarsi longer than the following joints together, clawjoint strongly incrassate; prosternum narrow, flavous, abdomen of the same colour.

Smaller and much narrower in shape than *H. nigripennis* Jac. likewise from Sumatra, the head and legs black as well as the breast, the antennae of different structure etc.

From Soekaranda.

Hyphasis biplagiata sp. n.

Below and the femora flavous, the antennae (the basal two joints excepted) and the tibiae and tarsi more or less black, head and thorax fulvous, impunctate, elytra extremely minutely punctured, piceous, each with an illdefined spot below the shoulders, fulvous.

Length $4^1/_2$ -5 mill.

Of broadly ovate shape, the head impunctate, fulvous, the frontal elevations strongly raised, the clypeus very acutely carinate between the antennae, eyes very large, antennae extending beyond the middle of the elytra, black, the first two joints fulvous, third and following joints of nearly equal length, slightly widened; thorax rather more than twice as broad as long, the sides evenly rounded, narrowly margined, the anterior angles slightly produced; the surface impunctate, fulvous, scutellum obscure fulvous, elytra only visibly punctured when seen under a strong lens, nearly black, with a rather obscure fulvous small spot of elongate shape, immediately below the shoulders, elytral epipleurae fulvous, very broad and concave; posterior femora very strongly incrassate, obscure fuscous at the apex, tibiae and tarsi piceous, the first joint of the posterior tarsi as long as the following two joints together.

Soekaranda and Liangagas.

Distinct in its coloration from any of its allies.

Acrocrypta Duvivieri sp. n.

Fulvous, terminal joints of the antennae black, the last flavous, thorax nearly impunctate, elytra purplish or violaceous, strongly and closely punctured, the punctures partly arranged in rows.

Length 5 mill.

Head fulvous, impunctate, frontal tubercles small, oblique, clypeus broad, antennae short and robust, black, the lower three joints fulvous, the others strongly widened and pubescent, the last joint flavous, thorax three times broader than long, the sides straight, the anterior angles obliquely thickened, posterior margin strongly rounded, the disc with some very fine punctures, irregularly placed, scutellum fulvous, elytra rounded and convex, strongly and closely punctured, the punctures partly arranged in rows, the last interstice at the sides obsoletely longitudinally costate; below and the legs fulvous.

Hab. Perak, also Isle Bedjo (my collection). Soekaranda, Liangagas, Sumatra (Dohrn).

Distinguished from *A. purpurea* Baly by the fulvous head, thorax and under side. In some specimens the elytra are much more finely punctured, but I can see no other differences and it is probably sexual.

Acrocrypta gibbosa sp. n.

Very convex and widened medially, fulvous, antennae black, the basal joints fulvous, the last flavous, thorax impunctate, elytra purplish blue, finely and moderately closely punctured.

Length 8 mill.

Head impunctate, fulvous, the frontal elevations flat and broad, bounded behind by narrow oblique grooves, clypeus very broad, impunctate, palpi strongly swollen, antennae with the lower five joints fulvous, the following five black, the apical one flavous, third joint elongate, as long as the first; thorax three times broader than long, strongly widened at the middle, the posterior margin rounded and sinuate, the anterior angles thickened, acute, the surface entirely impunctate, scutellum black, elytra distinctly widened at the middle, purplish blue, finely and moderately closely punctured, their apex nearly impunctate, the epipleurae very broad and concave, below and the legs fulvous, impunctate; prosternum very narrow, longitudinally sulcate.

Soekaranda.

This handsome and rather large species has almost the shape of a *Coccinella*, the elytra being strongly widened medially;

it is a larger insect than the preceding one and the elytral punctuation is finer in all specimens.

Chaloenus latifrons Westw.

The specimens obtained at Soekaranda by Dr. Dohrn agree very nearly with Westwood's description, but differ in having the clypeus blackish, not yellowish, the eyes in the male are also rather prominent but not anything like those in *C. oculatus*.

Chaloenus abdominalis sp. n.

Fulvous, the antennae (the apical joints excepted) the tibiae and tarsi and the abdomen black, thorax impunctate, elytra greenish-aeneous, punctured within the basal depression only.

Length 6 mill.

Mas. Head perpendicular, pale fulvous, the eyes prominent, the clypeus triangular, piceous, with a central longitudinal and deep lateral grooves, impunctate, antennae extending beyond the middle of the elytra, black, the apical three joints pale yellowish, basal joint long, its apex suddenly thickened, second short, the third and fourth more elongate, nearly equal, the following joints shorter and broader, the terminal three very short; thorax more than twice as broad as long, rather convex, the sides feebly rounded, the surface impunctate, reddish-fulvous, scutellum fulvous, elytra with the usual deep basal depression, the latter with a few punctures, a short row of punctures also placed within the shoulders to the base, rest of the surface impunctate, very shining, greenish-bronze colour, below and the femora fulvous, the tibiae and the tarsi as well as the abdomen blackish.

Soekaranda.

This species certainly differs considerably from its allies in the structure of the antennae, which have the third and fourth joints nearly equal while in the others the third joint is very elongate; the colour of the abdomen further separates the present insect of which I seem to have the sexes before me, as in the female the antennae are shorter and the third and fourth joints still shorter than in the male, the eyes are also scarcely so prominent.

Another closely allied species is the following.

Chaloenus semipunctata sp. n.

Piceous, the head, antennae, thorax and the femora fulvous, thorax impunctate, elytra nearly black, scarcely depressed below the base, with short rows of punctures not extending below the middle, third and fourth joints of the antennae equal.

Length 6 mill.

Fem.? Head impunctate, fulvous, the clypeus thickened, without grooves but with an acute central ridge at its upper portion, eyes not prominent, antennae entirely fulvous, of the same structure as in the preceding species; thorax likewise of similar shape and impunctate, scutellum black, elytra scarcely depressed below the base, piceous, the latter impunctate, the disc with three short rows of punctures not extending beyond the middle, a fourth row placed within the shoulders and extending to the base, below and the tibiae and tarsi black.

Hab. West-Sumatra (my collection).

Although I only possess a single apparently female specimen of this species, it differs so entirely in the fulvous antennae and their equal third and fourth joints, in the absence of an elytral basal depression, the presence of short rows of punctures and in the dark breast and abdomen, that there is no doubt of its specific distinction.

Chaloenus subcostatus sp. n. (Fig. 8).

Flavous, antennae piceous, the penultimate two joints whitish, thorax impunctate, transversely sulcate, elytra aeneous, deeply foveolate punctate, the interstices at the sides longitudinally costate, tibiae and tarsi fuscous.

Length 5 mill.

Closely allied to *C. aeneipennis* Jac. likewise from Sumatra, but with differently coloured antennae and sculptured elytra; the head impunctate, fulvous, the eyes not prominent, the clypeus thickened with a central longitudinal ridge, antennae slender, black, the basal three joints more or less fulvous, the ninth and tenth joints whitish or fulvous, basal joint very elongate, thickened at its apex, third and following joints gradually diminishing in length; thorax short, transverse, constricted at the base, the anterior angles thickened, the disc transversely sulcate, impunctate and shining, fulvous, scutellum aeneous; elytra much wider at the base than the thorax, greenish-aeneous, the entire disc impressed with deep foveolate punctures, the interstices irregularly rugose and transversely reticulate, the sides with two or three costae which are joined at their apex, below and the femora fulvous, the tibiae and tarsi blackish.

Soekarauda.

There were five specimens of this species obtained by Dr. Dohrn, and although, as already remarked the species is closely allied to *C. aeneipennis*, the totally different sculpturing of the elytra which are in consequence less shining than in that species, will at once distinguish *C. subcostatus*, but it is not impossible that the latter may represent the female of the first named insect.

Chaloenus oculatus sp. n. (Fig. 7).

Testaceous, antennae (the apical three joints excepted) tibiae and tarsi piceous, thorax impunctate, elytra metallic dark green, the base deeply depressed, punctured within the depression only.

Mas. Head with enormously protruding eyes, placed on lateral projections, lower portion of the face perpendicularly flattened, bisulcate.

Length 7 mill.

Head testaceous, impunctate, the extreme vertex piceous, the eyes protruding beyond the thorax, placed at the end of lateral projections, lower portion perpendicular, flat, furnished with two oblique grooves, antennae extending to the middle of the elytra, nearly black, the apical three joints whitish, basal joint extremely long, suddenly thickened at the apex, second short, third joint three times longer than the preceding, the following joints gradually shortened, thorax three times broader than long, the sides rounded before the middle, the angles rather oblique, the surface convex, impunctate, testaceous, elytra greenish-aeneous, deeply depressed below the base, the depression with a few punctures, indicating rows, rest of the surface impunctate, below and the legs testaceous, the tibiae and tarsi piceous.

Soekaranda.

Of this species, greatly distinguished by the extraordinary development of the lateral portion of the head, I possess a single specimen from Sumatra; although allied to *C. latifrons* Westw. the head, antennae and the underside are of different coloration and the position of the eyes is unique amongst the whole of the *Phytophaga*, resembling very much the same organs in the Crabs amongst the Crustacea. The female is unfortunately unknown to me.

Luperomorpha sumbaensis sp. n.

Black, shining, the anterior legs more or less piceous or fulvous, thorax impunctate, elytra extremely minutely punctured.

Length 3 mill.

Head black, impunctate, the frontal tubercles small, transverse, clypeus swollen with a highly raised central ridge, antennae long and robust, black, the lower three joints dark fulvous, second and third joints very small, subequal, fourth very elongate, the intermediate joints widened, thorax scarcely one half broader than long, the sides straight, the anterior angles thickened, the posterior ones obliquely rounded, the surface impunctate, black, shining, scutellum broad, elytra extremely finely and somewhat closely punctured, shining, black.

Sumba Island.

Closely allied to *L. trivialis* Weise from China and entirely resembling it in its coloration, but the upper surface is not alutaceous as Weise describes his species, and the thorax is impunctate. the elytra also are very finely punctured and shining.

Docemasia gen. n.

Body narrowly elongate. the antennae very long and filiform. the second and third joint very small. palpi incrassate at the penultimate joint. thorax subquadrate without sulcus. the posterior angles rounded. scutellum triangular. elytra wider at the base than the thorax. irregularly punctured. metallic, their epipleurae extremely narrow below the middle. posterior femora incrassate, tibiae non-sulcate, all armed with a small spine. the first joint of the posterior tarsi as long as the following joints together, claws appendiculate, prosternum scarcely visible between the coxae. the anterior cavities closed.

The small insect for which this genus is proposed. has the general appearance of a species of *Longitarsis:* the structural characters which distinguish the present genus. are the long antennae with their very short second and third joints. the nearly invisible prosternum and the closed anterior coxal cavities; the posterior femora are very distinctly incrassate, leaving no doubt as to the proper place of the genus among the *Halticinae*, where it may perhaps best be placed near *Cerotrus* Jac. which has likewise very short second and third joints of the antennae. but differs in the strongly transverse thorax and other details.

Docemasia caerulea sp. n.

Below black, above metallic dark blue, thorax very sparingly and finely punctured, elytra rather strongly and closely punctate. the base of the tibiae fulvous.

Length 3 mill.

Head with a few very minute punctures. dark blue. the frontal elevations in shape of narrow transverse ridges. clypeus distinctly raised between the antennae, palpi robust. eyes large, antennae extending to the apex of the elytra; black. the first joint fulvous at its extreme base. the second and third joint very small, the others elongate, of nearly equal length; thorax subquadrate, about one half broader than long, the posterior angles rounded, the sides straight, the surface with a few very fine punctures, scutellum broad, bluish; elytra dark blue or greenish, rather strongly punctured; below and the legs black, the coxae and the base of the tibiae fulvous.

Soekaranda and Liangagas.

Gallerucinae.

Oides pallidicornis sp. n.

Head, the breast and the legs black, antennae (the basal joint excepted) flavous, thorax and elytra testaceous or flavous, the former impunctate, the latter with irregular double and single rows of deep punctures, abdomen spotted with black.

Length 9—10 mill.

This species agrees entirely with *O. pectoralis* Cl. (*nigripes* Jac.) in colour and punctuation, but seems to differ constantly in the pale flavous antennae (these are black in *O. pectoralis*) which have only a black spot at the upper side of the basal joint; I can find no other charakters of distinction, but all the specimens from Sumatra show this difference and as there are no intermediate stages before me, I must look upon this species as a distinct one or at least as a local form. *O. nigripes* is moreover found in India and seems to possess longer antennae.

Hab. Sumatra (my collection). Soekaranda (Dohrn).

Aulacophora terminata sp. n.

Flavous, thorax fulvous, finely punctured, the transverse sulcus straight, elytra black, shining, finely and closely punctured, the lateral margins near the apex and the latter flavous.

Mas. The intermediate lobe of the last abdominal segment flat.

Length 6 mill.

This is another of the smaller species of *Aulacophora* with black elytra for the greater part and closely allied to *A. apici-*

pennis Jac. It will only be necessary to point out the differences between the two species; in the present insect the antennae, which are flavous, extend to about the middle of the elytra, and have the third and fourth joints equal, in *A. apicipennis* the third joint is distinctly longer than the fourth, the thorax is more closely punctured in *A. terminata* and the elytra, instead of having a small flavous spot placed at the apical angle near the suture, have a narrow flavous stripe extending from the apex a little upwards along the sides; the sexual characters are also entirely different in the males of the two insects; the present one, instead of having the median lobe of the last abdominal segment deeply sulcate as in *A. apicipennis* has this portion nearly flat, the female has the apex of the corresponding segment entire.

Hab. Soekaranda.

Aulacophora Dohrni sp. n.

Black, the head and thorax fulvous, the antennae and the anterior legs flavous, elytra without basal depression, finely punctured, flavous, the base with a more or less broad transverse black band.

Length 6 mill.

Head impunctate, fulvous or flavous, the labrum black, antennae rather long, flavous, the lower two joints more shining than the others, third and fourth joint equal, thorax with the transverse sulcus straight and moderately deep, the disc impunctate, fulvous, scutellum black, elytra without basal depression slightly longitudinally sulcate near the suture, very finely punctured, flavous, the black band at the base generally extending to one third of their length, its posterior edge deeply concave near the sides, the underside and the legs black, the anterior femora and tibiae more or less flavous, last abdominal segment trilobate, the median lobe not sulcate.

Soekaranda, Liangagas.

This species seems certainly distinct from *A. rosea* Fab., *A. lata* Baly and *A. Gestroi* Jac.; it is smaller than either of them and the colour of the underside and legs is different; of the five specimens I have before me, only one has the black portion of the elytra extending beyond the middle in the others this colour occupies only the anterior third; the last abdominal segment in the male has its apex very obscurely indented at each side (this can only be seen with great attention and a strong lens), the male organ is long and slender, its apex strongly pointed; *A. rosea* is always larger, more brightly marked and the structure of the last abdominal segment in the male is different, its median lobe deeply sulcate; *A. bicolor* Web. is much larger and the labrum is concolorous with the face. Two specimens are also contained in the present collection, which agree in everything with the type of *A. Dohrni* except in having the scutellum, entire underside and the legs flavous, but whether they represent a variety or a distinct species, more material is necessary to settle this point.

Ozomena Dohrni sp. n.

Reddish-fulvous, antennae black, the basal two joints fulvous, the apical three, white, thorax subquadrate, bifoveolate, impunctate, elytra violaceous, closely punctured and finely rugose, without costae.

Length 6 mill.

♀. Head impunctate, transversely grooved between the eyes, clypeus with strongly raised central ridge, antennae closely pubescent, the basal two joints fulvous, the second one extremely small, the third to the eighth joints black, of equal length, the last three yellowish-white; thorax nearly as long as broad, subquadrate, more or less deeply bifoveolate, smooth and shining, scutellum black, elytra very closely and strongly punctured, the interstices finely transversely rugose, below and the legs fulvous or the tibiae and tarsi fuscous.

Soekaranda.

The subquadrate thorax (not longer than broad as in *O. impressa* Fab.) and the entire absence of any elytral costae will distinguish this species; the male. which probably differs in the structure of the antennae, is unknown to me.

The following species contained in my collection seems closely allied but distinct.

Ozomena viridipennis sp. n.

Below and the legs piceous. antennae black. the apical three joints yellowish. head fulvous. with metallic gloss. thorax bluish-black, bifoveolate. elytra metallic green. closely and strongly punctured. without costae (♀).

Length 6—7 mill.

Head impunctate, light or darker fulvous. with a more or less distinct metallic bluish gloss, labrum and palpi piceous, antennae rather short. black. pubescent. the third and following joints of nearly equal length, the apical three, yellowish white; thorax slightly broader than long. the margins straight. the surface impunctate. bifoveolate. the foveae nearly contiguous. metallic bluish black. scutellum black. elytra metallic dark green. closely and strongly punctured. the interstices everywhere finely rugose. below fulvous or piceous as well as the legs with a more or less distinct bluish tint.

West-Sumatra.

Of this species. two very nearly identical female specimens are contained in my collection. they differ so entirely in coloration from any other species of the genus, that I do not doubt their specific distinction. the colour of the underside and that of the legs in connection with the absence of elytral costae and the colour of the head will distinguish the species.

Ozomena intermedia sp. n.

Reddish-fulvous. the antennae black. the basal two joints fulvous. the 9th and 10th whitish. the 11th black. thorax bifoveolate, impunctate, elytra violaceous, greenish or blue, closely and strongly punctured with traces of feeble longitudinal costae.

Length 7 mill.

Soekarauda.

This *Ozomena* is again closely allied to *O. Dohrni*, *O. impressa* and especially so to *O. bodjoensis* Duviv. It will only be necessary to point out the differences: from the first named, the species differs in the longer antennae and their much more elongate joints as well as in their black apical joint and the traces of elytral costae, the species is also larger and broader in shape: *O. impressa* has the thorax longer than broad and the elytra distinctly costate: *O. bodjoensis* agrees in nearly every respect, but the head is described as having a deep subquadrate fovea at the vertex which is not the case here, and the elytra are given with distinct and posteriorly joined costae, even more pronounced than in *O. impressa*. On the contrary all the specimens to the number of five agree in having the elytra closely and strongly punctured in somewhat irregular double rows which are feebly divided by indications, not real costae. All the specimens seem to belong to the female sex and as Duvivier had the same sex before him of his species, they cannot be identical: the last four joints of the antennae in *O. intermedia* are rather more elongate than the others with the exception of the third joint. *O. Modiglianii* Jac. has entirely black antennae and irregularly punctured elytra.

Xenoda parvula sp. n.

Pale testaceous, finely pubescent, the intermediate joints of the antennae fuscous, thorax impunctate, transversely sulcate, elytra closely pubescent, finely rugosely punctured, tibiae and tarsi fuscous.

Mas. The eighth joint of the antennae enormously thickened and elongate.

Fem. The same joint less thickened but distinctly elongate.

Length 5 mill.

Head impunctate, shining, pale fulvous or testaceous, the frontal elevations strongly raised, clypeus triangular, convex, palpi incrassate at the penultimate joint, the antennae robust, the basal and the apical three joints testaceous, the others fuscous, first joint robust, curved, second very small, moniliform, third twice as long, the following joints still longer, the eighth subcylindrical, very strongly widened and elongate, the ninth scarcely longer than the second joint, the tenth long and flattened, the last more slender and elongate; thorax very short, nearly three times broader than long, the sides straight, feebly narrowed at the base, the disc transversely sulcate impunctate, elytra finely rugose, clothed with fine whitish and rather long pubescence, legs slender, flavous like the under surface, the tibiae and tarsi blackish.

Soekaranda.

This small species agrees in all principal characters with the other members of the genus, but the antennae are differently structured; there is only a single male specimen contained in this collection and not in a very good condition, but sufficient to show the differences from the typical forms which generally have the third and following joints of the antennae greatly developed and often furnished with a spine; the present insect resembles in size *X. basalis* Jac. but differs in its entirely pale coloration and the structure of the antennae, this applies also to *X. pallida* Jac. which is besides of three times larger size; there is a general appearance of all the species of *Xenoda* by which they may be mostly recognized, that is the very short, transverse and sulcate thorax.

Xenoda spinicornis Baly.

I think, there is not much doubt, that Duvivier has described the female of this species as *Theopea Weyersi* (Bull. Soc. Ent. Belg. 1885): his description at all events and especially the short, transverse and sulcate thorax agrees entirely with Baly's species. I know, moreover, of no true species of *Theopea (Ozomena)* in which the elytra are pubescent.

Sastra apicicornis sp. n. (Fig. 14).

Dark blue, antennae black, the apical three joints yellowish-white, head and thorax rugose, the latter deeply bisulcate, elytra purplish, finely rugose and pubescent, tibiae and tarsi black.

Length 6 mill.

Of elongate shape, the head strongly rugose, with a central longitudinal groove, frontal elevations very narrow, transverse, antennae long and slender, black, the apical three joints yellowish-white, third joint very elongate, twice as long as the fourth, this and the following joints equal; thorax transverse, the sides straight at the base, slightly rounded before the middle, the angles feebly tuberculate, the surface closely and strongly punctured, dark metallic blue, the disc deeply transversely sulcate anteriorly, the sulcus interrupted in the middle, the base with another short transverse triangular fovea, scutellum broad, opaque, elytra finely rugose and wrinkled, purplish, sparingly pubescent; below dark blue, finely pubescent, tibiae and tarsi black, the first joint of the posterior tarsi as long as the following three joints together, claws bifid, anterior coxal cavities open.

Soekaranda, Liangagas.

Emathea intermedia sp. n. (Fig. 15).

Fulvous, the tibiae and tarsi more or less piceous, thorax strongly transverse, impunctate, elytra strongly widened posteriorly, dark violaceous, finely and closely punctured.

Length 6—9 mill.

Of strongly widened shape posteriorly, the head fulvous, impunctate, the frontal elevations broad and flat, clypeus distinctly raised, broad, antennae filiform, entirely fulvous or flavous, the third joint double the length of the second, much shorter than the fourth joint; thorax more than twice as broad as long, the sides straight, the anterior angles oblique, anterior margin concave, the sides with a narrow margin, the surface entirely impunctate, fulvous, scutellum piceous; elytra very feebly depressed below the base very finely and rather closely punctured, dark violaceous or purplish, below and the legs fulvous or flavous, the tibiae and tarsi more or less piceous or black.

Soekaranda.

Closely allied to *E. fulvicornis* Jac. but distinguished by the fine elytral punctuation, also by the broader frontal elevations and clypeus, the colour of the antennae separates the species from the other members of the genus, but their structure does not differ from those of the genus *Antipha* although the widened posterior shape agrees with *Emathea*.

Cynorta pallipes sp. n.

Black, head, thorax and legs pale fulvous, thorax bifoveolate, impunctate, elytra bright metallic green, strongly and closely punctured, extreme apex finely impunctate, sparingly pubescent.

Length 4 mill.

Head impunctate, transversely grooved between the eyes, the frontal elevations and the clypeus strongly raised, palpi thickened at the penultimate joint, antennae long and slender, black, the basal joint pale below, the third and following joints of nearly equal length; thorax subquadrate, slightly broader than long, the sides straight, slightly narrowed at the base, the disc deeply bifoveolate, impunctate, pale fulvous, scutellum black; elytra wider at the base than the thorax, deeply and closely punctured, bright metallic green, the interstices somewhat convex and transverse, the apex much more finely punctured and furnished with single hairs, legs pale flavous, the first joint of the posterior tarsi elongate.

Soekaranda.

This small species agrees in coloration with *C. capitata* Jac. and *C. monstrosa* Jac. also from Sumatra, but the deep and strong as well as close elytral punctuation and the small size distinguish it: there are only two specimens before me, glued to a card and I am unable to say anything about the sex, but in the two allied species mentioned above the head in the male insect is deeply excavate.

Galerucella inconspicua sp. n.

Obscure brownish-fuscous, finely pubescent, the antennae, tibiae and tarsi black, thorax impunctate, obsoletely depressed, elytra opaque, convex, very finely and closely punctured.

Length 7 mill.

Of convex, posteriorly slightly widened shape, entirely opaque and finely pubescent, the head impunctate, the frontal elevations flattened, elongate and pointed, the clypeus strongly raised in shape of a transverse ridge, eyes round, rather large, antennae not quite extending to the middle of the elytra, robust, black, the lower three joints dark fulvous, the third joint double as long as the second and one half longer than the fourth joint, terminal joints rather thickened and slightly shorter; thorax twice as broad as long, the sides obsoletely angulate before the middle, the surface with a central groove and very obsoletely depressed at the sides, of a dull opaque appearance, impunctate and finely pubescent, scutellum large, its apex truncate, elytra wider at the base than the thorax, very closely and finely punctured, the punctures rather more distantly placed at the anterior portion, elytral epipleurae broad at the base, concave, absent near the apex, below and the legs dark fulvous, the tibiae and tarsi black, the first joint of the posterior tarsi as long as the following two joints together, claws bifid, the anterior coxal cavities open.

Hab. Sumatra (Wallace) my collection.

Sastroides crassipalpis sp. n.

Obscure testaceous, finely pubescent, thorax glabrous, with three impressions, strongly and sparingly punctured, elytra broad and convex, rather dilated, very finely and closely punctured, clothed with grey pubescence, palpi very robust.

Length 9—10 mill.

Head glabrous, finely rugosely punctured at the vertex, the middle less closely so, frontal elevations as well as the clypeus strongly raised, last joint of the palpi strongly incrassate, eyes large, antennae extending slightly beyond the middle of the elytra, testaceous, the third joint very elongate, one half longer than the fourth, terminal joints shorter than the fourth joint, thorax at least twice as broad as long, the sides rounded before the middle, slightly constricted at the base, the posterior angles rather oblique, anterior angles tuberculiform, the disc with a lateral transverse and a basal longitudinal depression, shining and glabrous, sparingly but strongly punctured, scutellum broad, its apex rounded, elytra rather dilated posteriorly, pale fuscous or testaceous very finely and closely punctured and clothed with fine grey pubescence, the sides with a rather broadly reflexed and more strongly punctured margin, their epipleurae broad, concave and continued to the apex, below nearly glabrous, the legs slender, tibiae unarmed, the first joint of the posterior tarsi as long as the following two joints together, claws bifid, the anterior coxal cavities open.

Soekaranda.

Of this species, there are seven specimens before me, all of a fuscous grey colour, and of robust shape; in a former paper of mine on *Phytophaga* from Burma (Genoa Annals) I have already referred to the present species of which I however can find no description and must assume that I have overlooked to describe it. *S. unicolor* Jac. likewise from Sumatra exactly resembles the present insect but must I think find its place in another genus, since the palpi are slender and the elytral epipleurae indistinct below the middle, the thorax is likewise of other shape. *S. bimaculata* Jac. is of nearly similar appearance, but the thorax is longer, without the oblique posterior angles and is strongly and rather closely punctured, the elytra have also a blue round spot placed near the middle.

Sastroides fuscipennis sp. n.

Below testaceous, the antennae, tibiae and tarsi blackish, thorax flavous, strongly punctured and deeply impressed, elytra fuscous, finely rugose-punctate and clothed with greyish pubescence. Length 5 mill.

Head flavous, finely rugose, the frontal elevations small but distinct, clypeus strongly raised, labrum piceous, palpi strongly incrassate, eyes large, antennae extending to the middle of the elytra, black, the basal joint flavous below, third joint distinctly longer than the fourth; thorax twice as broad as long, the sides angulate before the middle, constricted at the base, the angles distinct, the disc with a deep lateral and a triangular basal depression or fovea, very strongly and closely punctured, flavous, shining, scutellum broad, fuscous, pubescent, elytra very closely and finely rugose-punctate, fuscous, closely covered with short greyish pubescence, their epipleurae broad and continued below the middle, underside and legs testaceous, closely pubescent, the anterior four tibiae and the tarsi piceous, the metatarsus of the posterior legs scarcely longer than the second joint, claws bifid, the anterior coxal cavities open.

Soekaranda and Liangagas.

The general appearance of this species is much like that of a *Galerucella* but the incrassate palpi and long third joint of the antennae places it in the present genus.

Sastracella gen. n.

Body ovate, pubescent, palpi and antennae filiform, the third joint of the latter elongate, thorax transverse, the sides rounded, the surface deeply depressed at the sides and at the base, elytra finely rugose and pubescent, their epipleurae indistinct below the middle, tibiae unarmed, longitudinally channelled, the metatarsus of the posterior legs as long as the following joints together, claws bifid, the anterior coxal cavities open.

It is necessary to erect this genus for the reception of some species of ovate, more or less dilated shape which are closely allied to the genus *Sastra* but differ in the more transversely shaped thorax and its rounded sides and in the absent elytral epipleurae below the middle, also in the long metatarsus of the posterior legs. In this genus must be placed *Sastra unicolor* Jac. and *S. fulvipennis* Jac.

Sastracella sumatrana sp. n.

Testaceous, the tibiae and tarsi black, thorax transverse, with three fovea, sparingly punctured, elytra black or fuscous, finely punctured and pubescent.

Length 6 mill.

Head rugosely punctured, the frontal elevations transverse, strongly raised, clypeus rather broad, palpi filiform, eyes very large, antennae testaceous or fulvous, nearly extending to the apex of the elytra, the third joint one third longer than the fourth, terminal joints shorter than the preceding ones; thorax twice as broad as long, the sides rounded, the posterior margin somewhat sinuate, the surface deeply transversely depressed at the sides and at the base, testaceous, shining, strongly but not closely punctured, scutellum broad, testaceous, elytra nearly black or fuscous, finely rugose, closely covered with grey pubescence, below and the legs testaceous, finely pubescent, the knees, tibiae and tarsi blackish.

Soekaranda.

Niasia caeruleipennis sp. n. (Fig. 6).

Head bluish black, antennae black, the basal joint of the latter and the thorax flavous, impunctate, elytra metallic blue, finely and very closely punctured, below piceous, legs flavous.

Mas.? Antennae with the 8th and 9th joints strongly dilated.

Length 4 mill.

Of ovate, convex shape, the head impunctate, bluish-black, transversely grooved between the eyes, the frontal elevations very broad, nearly contiguous, clypeus triangularly raised, eyes very large, antennae closely approached at the base, black, the lower three joints flavous, first joint elongate and thickened, second short, third nearly twice as long, the following four joints very short, nearly moniliform, the eighth triangularly dilated, the ninth longer, also very strongly thickened, tenth cylindrical, elongate, as well as the terminal one which is strongly pointed, thorax twice as broad as long, of equal width, the sides feebly rounded, the surface rather convex, impunctate flavous, scutellum broad, piceous, elytra widened towards the middle, distinctly and very closely punctured, metallic blue, legs flavous, the breast and abdomen as well as the tarsi more or less piceous.

Liangagas, Soekaranda.

This is the second species of the genus originally described by me from Nias (Annali Mus. Genova 1889): it agrees entirely in structural characters with the type but differs totally in coloration and unless the Nias specimen should prove to be an entirely fulvous variety, the present species will be easily distinguished. I am at present unable to say whether the structure of the antennae is peculiar to the male sex only, not having enough material before me to decide this, but it is probable that the female possesses simple antennae.

Diorhabda robusta sp. n.

Very broad and robust, pale fuscous, finely pubescent, the antennae (the basal joints excepted) and the tibiae and tarsi black, thorax finely rugose-punctate without spots, elytra sculptured like the thorax and finely pubescent.

Length 10—12 mill.

Head finely rugose, without spots, the clypeus strongly raised, eyes large, frontal elevations obsolete, antennae short and robust, not extending to the middle of the elytra, black, the basal two joints testaceous, third and fourth joints equal, terminal joints shorter and thinner; thorax more than twice as broad as long, the sides widened at the middle and forming an obsolete angle, narrowed or constricted anteriorly, the anterior angles in shape of a small tubercle, the surface finely rugosely punctured, with a very shallow lateral and central depression, the interstices very sparingly pubescent, scutellum broad, its apex truncate; elytra very finely and closely rugose-punctate, and closely covered with short grey pubescence, their epipleurae broad and concave anteriorly, continued below the middle, tibiae black, unarmed, claws bifid, the anterior coxal cavities closed.

Soekaranda.

A species of very broad and robust appearance and clothed with very short pubescence which cannot be placed in *Galerucella* on account of the closed coxal cavities.

Metellus laevipennis Jac. (Fig. 12).

At the time of my description of this species (Genova Annali 1885) I only knew the male insect, which, like the type of the genus, is distinguished by having the third joint of the antennae strongly dilated and broadly flattened; Dr. Dohrn has now obtained besides this sex the females, which were captured at Soekaranda, which differ from the males, in having as usual, simple, filiform antennae, the third joint of which is slightly longer than the others; the head and thorax vary in colour from fulvous to piceous. Like so many other genera, the present genus is merely established on the male structural character of the antennae, as there is little else to distinguish it from *Dorydea* or *Platyxantha*, but it will at all events help in the classification of the species.

Metellus nigripennis sp. n.

Fulvous, the antennae, tibiae and tarsi fuscous, thorax impunctate, bifoveolate, elytra black, extremely finely punctured, depressed below the base.

Mas. The third joint of the antennae thickened, subcylindrical and elongate.

Fem. Antennae shorter, simple, fulvous.

Length 7 mill.

Head elongate, the vertex smooth and impunctate, fulvous, the clypeus swollen with a central ridge, very finely rugose and opaque, penultimate joint of the palpi incrassate, antennae in the male nearly extending to the apex of the elytra, fuscous, the basal joint fulvous below, short and thick, the second one extremely small, the third elongate, thickened, the upper edge slightly angulate near the base, the following two joints equal, of normal shape, the others more elongate, thorax one half broader than long, the sides widened before the middle, the angles distinct, the surface impunctate, fulvous, bifoveolate, scutellum blackish, large elytra distinctly depressed below the base, very finely and rather closely punctured, black, with a slight bluish gloss, their epipleurae broad and extending to the apex, legs slender, the tibiae unarmed, black, like the tarsi, and closed with fine yellowish pubescence, anterior coxal cavities closed.

Soekaranda.

Two species of this genus have been described up to the present, the generic name of *Neocharis*, first given to it by myself has been subsequently altered to *Metellus*, but Baly described the genus later again under the name of *Nacrea*, his species *N. maculata* is synonym with *Metellus fulvicollis* Jac. The present insect differs from both its allies in the differently structured third joint of the antennae and in the entirely black elytra; the female has simple and entirely fulvous antennae and resembles much a species of *Cynorta*, it is however a very much broader insect than any species of that genus, both in regard to the thorax and the elytra.

Platyxantha coxalis sp. n.

Terminal joints of the antennae, the body and legs black, thorax bifoveolate, fulvous, impunctate, elytra fulvous, closely and rather strongly punctured, the extreme base of all the femora flavous.

Mas. The terminal joints of the antennae thickened.

Length 8 mill.

Head elongate, impunctate, frontal elevations transverse, antennae extending to the middle of the elytra, black, the lower three or four joints fulvous, second joint very small, third as long as the first, the following joints slightly shorter, gradually thickened, terminal joint much longer than broad, thickened but pointed; thorax subquadrate; scarcely broader than long, the surface impunctate, fulvous, bifoveolate, scutellum broad, pale fulvous, elytra rather flattened, not depressed below the base, comparatively strongly and closely punctured, the punctuation rather finer towards the apex, below and the legs black, the abdomen finely pubescent, the base of the femora flavous, penis very short and broad, its apex broadly rounded.

Soekaranda.

Of this species there are apparently only male specimens before me which resemble in the structure of the antennae and in general coloration *P. apicalis* Baly; but in that species the last two joints of the antennae as well as the scutellum are black, only the elytra are less strongly punctured and the posterior tibiae have a styliform process which is absent in the present insect.

Platyxantha sumatrana sp. n. (Fig. 9).

Reddish fulvous, the antennae and legs flavous, thorax impunctate, bifoveolate, elytra finely and sparingly punctured, with a slight purplish gloss.

Mas. The intermediate joints of the antennae triangularly dilated, the terminal two joints slender, the posterior tibiae with a short styliform process.

Length 8 mill.

Head produced, fulvous, impunctate, acutely ridged between the antennae, labrum and palpi flavous, antennae nearly extending to the end of the elytra in the male, shorter in the female, flavous, the basal joint curved, the second very small, moniliform, the third and fourth elongate, equal, thickened at the apex, the following joints strongly triangularly dilated, the apex of each produced, the terminal two joints slender again; thorax subquadrate, narrowed at the base, the surface entirely impunctate, bifoveolate, fulvous, elytra wider at the base than the thorax, very feebly depressed below the base, finely punctured with some traces of longitudinal sulci near the sides in some specimens, of a reddish fulvous colour with a slight purplish gloss, below rather darker fulvous, smooth and shining, legs slender, flavous, the first joint of the posterior tarsi longer than the following joints together.

Liangagas.

In this species the antennae have no joints suddenly thickened like several others of the genus, but their intermediate joints are gradually widened, in other respects the species does not differ structurally from *Platyxantha*, in the female the antennae are entirely filiform and the posterior tibiae have no styliform process.

Platyxantha bifasciata sp. n. (Fig. 10).

Pale fulvous, the tibiae and the underside fuscous, thorax with a few minute punctures, bifoveolate, elytra very finely punctured, each elytron with a sinuate longitudinal fuscous band not extending to the apex but curving towards the suture, abdominal segments margined with flavous.

Mas. Antennae with the fourth to the eighth joints triangularly dilated, the ninth strongly thickened as well as the tenth, the latter shorter, the terminal joint elongate and slender.

Length 8 mill.

Soekaranda. (A single specimen).

In all the principal structural characters and in the shape this species agrees with the preceding ones, but the antennae differ again in having the ninth and tenth joints dilated, both are of semicircular shape and the tenth is shorter than the preceding joint; the species is the only one known to me having elytral stripes, these are of sinuate shape and suddenly turn to the suture near the apex, on this account the species will be easily recognized. Only a single male specimen was obtained.

Platyxantha monstrosa sp. n. (Fig. 11).

Below black, above dark fulvous, scutellum, the tibiae and tarsi blackish, thorax deeply bifoveolate, the foveae punctured, elytra extremely finely and sparingly punctured, abdominal segments margined with flavous.

Mas. Antennae with the ninth joint enormously dilated, the tenth, short and thick, subquadrate, terminal joint wanting.

Length 8 mill.

Soekaranda.

Again of similar shape and structure of the preceding species, but the antennae with the ninth joint extremely large and widened, more so than in any of the allied forms, the shape of this joint is something between a hatchet and a club, the tenth is also very thick but less than half the length of the preceding one, the third and fourth joints are nearly equal, elongate, the following are triangularly dilated and shorter; only a single male specimen is before me; the terminal joint of the antennae is probably elongate again as is generally the case. In *Dorydea insignis* Baly the antennae have the corresponding joints likewise enormously widened but their shape is quite different and they are also deeply hollowed out.

Platyxantha nigrolimbata sp. n.

Head and thorax fulvous, the antennae, the breast and the tibiae and tarsi black, thorax bifoveolate, impunctate, elytra extremely finely punctured, black or piceous, the disc more or less broadly flavous.

Var. Elytra flavous, the base and the apical margins narrowly black.

Length 6 mill.

Head impunctate, fulvous, the clypeus narrowly thickened, flavous, labrum and palpi piceous, antennae very thin and slender.

black, with fringes of rather long black hairs at the edges of the joints, the third joint the longest, the following slightly shorter, the basal joint elongate and thickened, thorax one half broader than long, fulvous, the sides slightly constricted at the base, the surface very shining, impunctate, deeply bifoveolate, scutellum black, elytra flattened, extremely finely punctured, the disc more or less broadly pale flavous, the base, sides and apex black; abdomen flavous, the breast, the apex of the femora and the tibiae and tarsi black, the metatarsus of the posterior legs as long as the following joints together, tibiae unarmed, the anterior coxal cavities closed.

Soekaranda.

The present insect resembles somewhat in coloration *Aenidea variabilis* Jac. (Ann. Mus. Civico Genova 1886), but the antennae in that species are quite differently structured and the general size is much larger besides other differences. In the present species the clypeus in all the specimens is bright flavous in contrast to the fulvous head; it is probable that the four specimens before are females, the abdomen is too much shrivelled to come to definite conclusion in that respect.

Haplosonyx batuensis Jac. (Fig. 13).

Several specimens from Soekaranda contained in this collection agree with those described by myself in the Annali di Genova 1897 from the island of Batu; a specimen from Soekaranda is figured.

Dorydea nigripennis Jac. (Fig. 16).

Dr. Dohrn obtained specimens of this species at Soekaranda: the typical form with black elytra was described by myself in the Genoa Annals 1896 from Si-Rambé in Sumatra: in the present collections some specimens have the elytra fulvous, but the structure of the antennae as shown in the figure is identical.

Monolepta rufipennis sp. n.

Black, the antennae flavous, thorax impunctate, elytra rufous, extremely closely and distinctly punctured.

Length 5 mill.

Head black, impunctate, the frontal elevations trigonate, contiguous, the eyes very large, rather closely approached, the antennae extending beyond the middle of the elytra, flavous, the basal two joints black, the third joint slightly longer than the second one, the fourth longer than the preceding two joints together, the fifth and following joints still more elongate; thorax about one half broader than long, the sides and the posterior margin rounded, the surface rather convex, black, impunctate and shining, scutellum fulvous, elytra convex, rather widened posteriorly, rufous, shining, very closely and rather strongly punctured, the punctures distinct to the apex, their epipleurae indistinct below the middle; below black or fulvous, the legs black, the first joint of the posterior tarsi very elongate.

Soekaranda, also Perak (my collection).

M. Allard has described a *Monolepta* from Malacca (*M. castanea*) with which I cannot identify the present species, as Allard gives the entire colour as black, excepting the elytra which are rufous, this would therefore apply also to the antennae which are not black but flavous in *M. rufipennis*. The elytral punctuation also is not arranged in rows anteriorly nor does it disappear towards the apex, as the above named author describes his species. The underside in the Sumatran specimen is fulvous, in the one from Perak nearly black, but no other differences are present.

Candezea C-album sp. n.

Flavous, the antennae, tibiae and tarsi black, head and thorax fulvous, the latter subquadrate, impunctate, elytra black, extremely finely punctured at the base, the middle of the disc of each with a c-shaped whitish band, the suture below the base deeply foveolate.

Length 5 mill.

Of convex, posteriorly widened shape, the head reddish-fulvous, impunctate, the lower portion rather flattened, eyes large, antennae long and slender, black, extending nearly to the apex of the elytra, the third joint one half longer than the second one, the others very long and thin; thorax not longer than broad, the sides straight, the angles oblique, the surface impunctate, reddish-fulvous, scutellum fulvous, elytra wider at the base than the thorax, convex, scarcely perceptibly punctured, black, the disc with a curved c-shaped yellowish-white stripe commencing below the base and extending to the middle of the suture, the including black space with a deep oblong fovea, elytral epipleurae continued below the middle, the underside and the base of the femora flavous, the rest of the legs black, the first joint of the posterior tarsi very long.

Liangagas and Soekaranda.

The elytral fovea in this species is probably peculiar to the male insect only, but is present in the four examples before me, the pattern of the elytra will distinguish the species at first sight.

Candezea circumducta sp. n.

Fulvous, the antennae and legs piceous, thorax impunctate, transverse, elytra extremely finely and closely punctured, black, the basal half in shape of a broad slightly curved band, surrounding the scutellum, yellowish-white, abdomen flavous, the breast blackish.

Mas.? The elytra with a sutural fovea below the base.

Length 4 mill.

Somewhat resembling the preceding species, but much smaller, the lower three joints of the antennae fulvous, the thorax one half broader than long, the angles not oblique and distinct, the surface very finely punctured; elytra punctured like the thorax, the entire anterior half occupied by a broad whitish band surrounding the scutellum and not extending to the lateral margins, leaving a narrow sutural space of the black ground colour.

Hab. Soekaranda.

The above differences will at once distinguish this species from *C. c-album*, the sutural fovea is also less deep. *C. discoidalis* Jac. from Perak again resembles the present insect but is generally larger and has the apical joints of the antennae flavous and the apex of the elytra fulvous.

Candezea laticornis sp. n.

Black, the thorax, abdomen and the femora flavous, elytra extremely minutely and closely punctured, black, a transverse band at the middle pale flavous; antennae with the intermediate joints widened and pubescent.

Length 5 mill.

Head black, impunctate, deeply transversely grooved between the eyes, the latter very large, antennae black, the second and third joints small, the fourth and following joints rather widened, pubescent, thorax about one half broader than long, its sides straight at the base, feebly rounded before the middle, the disc impunctate, flavous, elytra wider at the base than the thorax, black, very closely and finely punctured, the middle with a rather broad transverse yellowish-white band not quite extending to the lateral margins and of somewhat variable width, elytral epipleurae continued below the middle, the abdomen and the femora flavous, the tibiae and tarsi black, the metatarsus of the posterior legs very elongate.

Soekaranda, also Java, Borneo and Perak (my collection).

From all nearly similarly coloured species of the genus and of *Monolepta* the present one may be known by the structure and the pubescence of the antennae which somewhat resemble those of the genus *Arcastes*; the present species possesses however all the structural characters of *Candezea* and the closed anterior coxal cavities; the elytral pale band is however subject to variation in regard to its width in a longitudinal sense.

Candezea nigrilabrum sp. n.

Testaceous or flavous, the labrum and the scutellum black, head and thorax impunctate, elytra scarcely perceptibly punctured, the breast, tibiae and tarsi black.

Length 4 mill.

Head entirely impunctate, pale fulvous, the clypeus with a central ridge, labrum black, antennae extending to about the middle of the elytra, the lower joints pale fulvous, the others fuscous, basal joint long and curved, the second short, the third double the length, the others elongate, slightly longer than the third joint; thorax subquadrate, about one half broader than long, slightly constricted at the base, the margins nearly straight, the surface impunctate, coloured like the head, scutellum black, elytra wider at the base than the thorax and of paler colour, microscopically punctured, their epipleurae continued below the middle; abdomen and the femora flavous, the breast, tibiae and the tarsi black, metatarsus of the posterior legs elongate.

Soekaranda.

Of this small species two specimens are before me, one of them has a small elytral fovea below the base at the suture, probably a male character; the species may be known from its allies and those somewhat similarly coloured species of *Monolepta* by the system of coloration, notably the black breast, tibiae and tarsi.

Antipha Wallacei sp. n.

Head, thorax and the abdomen black, the antennae fulvous, elytra reddish-brown, finely and closely punctured, the apex black, thorax impunctate, legs fulvous or more or less black.

Length 6—7 mill.

Of the same coloration as so many other Sumatran *Phytophaga* but differing in detail from any of its congeners; the head in one specimen with two fulvous spots on the vertex, impunctate, the clypeus black, smooth and impunctate. the antennae flavous. the basal joint piceous (the fifth and rest of the joints wanting). thorax twice as broad as long. the sides straight. the anterior angles obliquely thickened. the surface obsoletely transversely depressed, black, shining and impunctate. scutellum fulvous; elytra with a very feeble depression below the base. rather strongly and closely punctured, reddish-fulvous. the apex to a small extend black; below fulvous. the legs and the abdomen black: in the other specimen the head is black with a faint trace of the fulvous spots. the third joint of the antennae is double the length of the second, the fourth joint more than twice the length of the third. the thorax has no depression and the elytra are more finely punctured and the legs are fulvous. Both specimens were obtained at Soekaranda and these differences are probably only sexual and the species subject to variation. *A. Wallacei* differs from *A. abdominalis* Jac. in the black abdomen, impunctate thorax and differently coloured elytra. from *A. variabilis* Jac. in the non pubescent elytra. fulvous breast etc. and from *A. bipartita* Jac. in being twice as large and in the black abdomen.

Macrima fuscolineata sp. n.

Testaceous, the breast and the abdomen more or less black. thorax subquadrate. bifoveolate. elytra very finely punctured. the lateral margin narrowly and a broad longitudinal stripe from the base to the apex. fuscous.

Var. The elytral stripes scarcely visible or more or less obsolete.

Length 8 mill.

Elongate and parallel. the head impunctate. the clypeus. and the frontal tubercles distinctly raised. antennae long and slender, testaceous, the second joint very small, the third and following joints elongate and equal, thorax subquadrate, narrowed at the base, the sides widened before the middle, the angles not produced, the surface shining and impunctate, rather deeply bifoveolate, elytra much wider at the base than the thorax, very finely and closely punctured, the interstices with traces of longitudinal costae, very indistinct in the male, more marked in the other sex, the disc with a rather broad fuscous band commencing at the middle of the base and extending nearly to the apex, the lateral margins likewise narrowly fuscous; elytral epipleurae broad, extending to the apex, the breast and abdomen black, the latter margined with flavous at each segment, the last entirely of that colour, legs testaceous, the first joint of the posterior tarsi longer than the following three joints together, claws appendiculate, the anterior coxal cavities closed, the last abdominal segment of the male incised at each side, the median lobe transverse, slightly concave, the male organ long and slender, parallel, the apex rounded and produced into a small point at the middle.

Soekaranda.

This species differs in coloration from its allies; the well marked specimens are therefore easily recognized, but the elytral stripe varies greatly in intensity and is scarcely perceptible in some instances. Whether *M. abdominalis* Jac. is really distinct from the present species or represents only the unicolorous variety I am unable to say, as I have not now the type before me. But my description speaks of the tibiae as being piceous and the elytra having a depression below the base, which is not the case in the seven specimens before me.

Macrima nigrolimbata sp. n.

Fulvous above, the antennae and the femora flavous, the breast and the abdomen partly black, thorax impunctate, deeply bifoveolate, elytra finely and closely punctured, fulvous, the suture and lateral margins narrowly black.

Mas. The posterior tibiae curved and dilated at the middle.

Length 7 mill.

This and the following species have been formerly looked upon by myself as varieties of *M. abdominalis* Jac., but more material which has come to hand since have convinced me, that they really represent distinct species. The head and thorax of the present insect do not differ from the other allied forms, the antennae are likewise long and slender and of flavous colour, all the joints with the exception of the small second one are elongate and nearly equal in length, the thorax has the foveae deep and nearly contiguous, the scutellum is black, the elytra have a slight depression below the base and are very finely and closely punctured, with very slight traces of longitudinal costae, the extreme sutural and lateral margins are more or less distinctly black, the breast and the greater part of the abdomen is of the latter colour, the femora and the apex of the abdomen is flavous or fulvous, the tibiae and tarsi fuscous.

Hab. Soekaranda, also Borneo (coll. Jacoby).

The male of this species may at once be distinguished by the dilated posterior tibiae; the last abdominal segment has the usual lateral incisions, the middle lobe being flat and of transverse shape; the female can only be separated from those of the other species by the colour of the elytra.

Macrima flavoplagiata sp. n.

Fulvous, the antennae and the legs flavous, the scutellum, breast and abdomen black, thorax impunctate, bifoveolate, elytra not perceptibly punctured, fulvous, the space surrounding the scutellum, flavous.

Length 7—8 mill.

Similar in shape and structure to the preceding species, the antennae extending below the middle of the elytra, flavous, the intermediate joints slightly curved, the thorax impunctate, bifoveolate and narrowed at the base; the elytra with a distinct basal depression with a few minute punctures at the base, the rest of the surface impunctate, dark fulvous, the space immediately round the scutellum flavous, the underside entirely black, the extreme apex of the last abdominal segment and the legs flavous; the male with the usual trilobate apex of the abdomen, the median lobe slightly concave.

Soekaranda also Perak (coll. Jacoby).

That this species is really distinct from the preceding is proved by the simple not dilated tibiae of the male, the nearly impunctate elytra, which show no traces of any costae and their different coloration; in some specimens the basal portion of the elytral suture is more or less blackish. I have examined eight specimens.

Euphymasia gen. n.

Body broadly ovately rounded, palpi filiform, antennae rather short and robust the second joint short the third and following joints but little larger, terminal joints more elongate; thorax transverse, short, without depressions, the basal margin with a very small, obsolete notch at each side; elytra irregularly punctured, their epipleurae very broad, continued to the apex, legs short and robust, the posterior femora slightly thickened, the four posterior tibiae mucronate; claws appendiculate, prosternum narrow, but distinct metasternum abruptly truncate, slightly raised anteriorly, the anterior coxal cavities closed.

This genus seems somewhat allied to *Nancita* Alld. and *Dorydia* Baly, but in the first named genus the palpi are thickened and the metatarsus of the posterior legs is shorter than the following two joints together (in the present genus, the first joint is as long as the following two joints), the metasternum is not mentioned in Allard's description; in *Doryida* the palpi are dilated, the antennae are filiform and their third joint is double as long as the preceding one there is also an absence of the short notches at the base of the thorax which are also to be found in *Solenia*

Stett. entomol. Zeit. 1889.

Jac. (*Euphyma* Baly). The genus seems to be a form of transition between the *Halticinae* and *Galerucinae* without the strongly developed posterior femora.

Euphymasia Dohrni sp. n. (Fig. 5).

Fulvous, with slight aeneous gloss, thorax scarcely perceptibly punctured, elytra convex, closely and finely punctured.

Length 9 mill.

Head flat impunctate, the frontal elevations narrowly oblique, bounded by grooves behind clypeus broad at its apex impunctate triangularly emarginate in front labrum with a row of deep punctures, mandibles robust and prominent palpi slender, the last joint acutely pointed, antennae not extending to the middle of the elytra, fulvous; thorax twice as broad as long, the sides very feebly rounded, the anterior margin nearly straight posterior margin rounded and produced at the middle, the surface extremely minutely punctured, scutellum broad, impunctate; elytra wider at the base than the thorax, more distinctly punctured than the thorax, the punctuation fine and very close, the surface with a slight metallic lustre; below and the legs fulvous, the apex of the tibiae clothed with fulvous pubescence.

Obtained in January at Soekaranda and Liangagas.

Pseudeustetha gen. n.

Body subquadrate-ovate pubescent, antennae short the intermediate joints widened, thorax transverse, the sides straight, the surface obsoletely bifoveolate, elytra closely and irregularly punctured and pubescent, their epipleurae continued below the middle legs unarmed the first joint of the posterior tibiae longer than the following joints together, claws appendiculate, prosternum narrow, convex, mesosternum perpendicularly truncate, the anterior coxal cavities closed.

This genus will enter the *Hylaspinae* of Chapuis' arrangement on account of its robust subquadrate shape and that of the mesosternum, which although not raised is truncate anteriorly and deflexed: from all the other genera placed in the present group, *Pseudeustetha* in distinguished by the pubescence of the entire upper surface and the long metatarsus of the posterior legs.

Pseudeustetha quadriplagiata sp. n.

Fulvous, the intermediate joints of the antennae black, thorax finely rugose punctate, pubescent, elytra very minutely punctured with larger punctures arranged in irregular rows, clothed with yellow pubescence, a large patch at the base and another near the apex black.

Length 8 mill.

Head with a few strigae and a fovea between the antennae, sparingly pubescent, eyes large, frontal elevations transverse, clypeus acutely raised, antennae extending a little below the base of the elytra, the lower three joints fulvous, the following five black, the ninth and tenth nearly white, the apical joint black again, third joint more than twice as long as the second, the fourth joint as long as the third, the following three widened, pubescent, the apical joints slender again; thorax twice as broad as long, slightly narrowed in front, the sides straight, oblique, the anterior angles obliquely thickened, the surface finely rugose, with an obsolete fovea at each side, the disc clothed with yellow pubescence, scutellum broad, elytra convex, scarcely broader than the thorax, clothed with long yellow pubescence, fulvous, the punctuation very fine with indistinct rows of larger punctures, the base with a large subquadrate black patch not extending to the basal margin and another smaller patch placed near the apex, below and the legs fulvous.

Soekaranda.

Two specimens only are before me, the black patches of the elytra are partly obscured by the pubescence.

Notes on previously described species.

Cleorina nigrita Jac.

I find that I have described two species under this name, one in the Stettiner Zeitung 1895 and the other in the Genoa Annals 1896. For the latter species I substitute therefore the name of *Cleorina sumatrana*.

Pachnephorus plagiatus Jac.

This species seems identical with *P. Bretinghami* Baly from India.

Sphaerometopa obsoleta Jac., S. 4-punctata Jac., S. intermedia Jac.

These three species must be placed in *Acrocrypta* on account of the closed anterior cavities.

Explanation of plate.

No. 1. *Lema verrucosa.*
2. *Temnaspis nigricollis.*
3. „ *Dohrni.*
4. *Aspidolopha imperialis* var.
5. *Euphymasia Dohrni.*
6. *Niasia caeruleipennis.*
7. *Chaloenus oculatus.*
8. „ *subcostatus.*
9. *Platyxantha sumatrana.*
10. „ *bifasciata.*
11. „ *monstrosa.*
12. *Metellus laevipennis.*
13. *Haplosonyx batuensis.*
14. *Sastra apicicornis.*
15. *Emathea intermedia.*
16. *Dorydia nigripennis.*

Verzeichniss der Phytophagen von Deli,

zusammengestellt von **H. Dohrn.**

In der Einleitung zu der vorstehenden Arbeit meint Herr Jacoby, es sei nicht nöthig, ein Verzeichniß der sämmtlichen von mir in Deli gesammelten Arten der von ihm bearbeiteten Gruppen der Phytophagen zu geben, welche schon anderweit beschrieben seien. Ich kann diese Ansicht nicht theilen, einmal, weil es an sich wichtig ist, die geographische Verbreitung genau festzustellen, um die Verwandtschaft der Sumatraner Fauna nach dem Festlande hin ebensowohl, wie nach den anderen malayischen Regionen zu detailliren, zweitens um auch für Sumatra selbst zu einer Uebersicht und Characteristik der faunistisch zu scheidenden Gebiete zu gelangen. Bei einem Lande, welches sich über 10 Breitengrade von Norden nach Süden erstreckt, welches in seiner ganzen Länge von einem hohen Gebirge durchzogen wird, ist als sicher anzunehmen, daß sowohl horizontal wie vertikal solche Gebiete vorhanden sind. Wenn nun auch bisher das entomologische Material aus einzelnen Gegenden recht lückenhaft ist, so glaube ich doch jetzt schon auf die große Verschiedenheit der Ausbeute aus zwei Lokalsammlungen hinweisen zu können, welche dort in der Entfernung von nur wenigen Meilen, aber in einer Höhendifferenz von rund 3000 Fuß gemacht sind, deren beide eine ziemlich große Artenzahl enthalten. Es sind das die Sammlung, welche Modigliani am Südrande des Toba See's gemacht hat, und die meinige aus dem Flachlande von Deli. Die Erstere ist von Jacoby in den Annali del Museo Civico di Storia naturale di Genova 1896 pag. 377 ff. vollständig mit 139 Arten verzeichnet; die in derselben Arbeit enthaltenen weiteren 25 Arten sind ohne genauere Angabe des Fundortes oder von der Westküste. Meine Ausbeute ist viel größer, was erklärlich ist, da auf ihre Erlangung längere Zeit verwendet ist und da vielleicht auch der Artenreichthum des heißen Tieflandes ein größerer ist. Unter den 271 von Herrn Jacoby bestimmten Arten befinden sich nur 32, welche auch Modigliani gebracht hat. Dazu kommt, daß die Familien und Gattungen höchst ungleichmäßig vertreten zu sein scheinen. *Sagra* fehlt bei Modigliani. *Crioceriden* sind durch eine Art vertreten, ebenso *Aulacophora*, während in dem Tieflande von ersteren 15, von letzterer 20 Arten vorhanden sind.

Im folgenden Verzeichniß der von mir gesammelten Arten habe ich die auch vom Toba-See gebrachten mit einem Sternchen bezeichnet.

Sagrinae.

Sagra.

borneensis Jac.

femorata Drury.

Criocerinae.

Lema.

Beccarii Jac.

coromandeliana Lac.

cyanipennis Fabr.

Dohrni Jac.

femorata Germ.

Gestroi Jac.

haematomelas Lac.

palpalis Lac.

quadripunctata Oliv.

separata Jac.

striatopunctata Lac.

verrucosa Jac. n. sp.

Crioceris.

impressa Fabr.

quadripustulata Lac.

semipunctata Fab.

Megalopodinae.

Temnaspis.

Dohrni Jac. n. sp.

nigricollis Jac. n. sp.

Clytrinae.

Aspidolopha.

Buqueti Lac.

capitata Jac. n. sp.

imperialis Baly.

Gynandrophthalma.

malayana Baly.

occipitalis Jac. n. sp.

Cryptocephalinae.

Bucharis.

*constricticollis Jac.

laevicollis Jac. n. sp.

Melixanthus.

bimaculicollis Baly.

Cryptocephalus.

apicipennis Baly.

cinnabarinus Suffr.

Gemmingeri Jac.

suspectus Baly.

Lamprosominae.

Oomorphus.

caeruleus Jac. n. sp.

Eumolpinae.

Nodostoma.

Bohemani Baly.

Dohrni Jac. n. sp.

frontale Baly.
multicostatum Jac.
nigripes Baly.
*nigrosuturatum Jac.
Staudingeri Jac.

Nodina.
fulvicollis Jac. n. sp.
*fulvitarsis Jac.
multicostata Jac.
robusta Jac.

Aulexis.
elongata Jac.
longicornis Jac. n. sp.
*Wallacei Baly.

Callisina.
fasciata Baly.

Sc.lodonta.
nitidula Baly.

Aoria.
Bowringi Baly.
nigripes Baly.

Phytorus.
dilatatus Jac.
nigrolimbatus Lef.
simplex Lef.

Pachnephorus.
Bretinghami Baly.

Apolepis.
atra Lef.

Tricliona.
fasciata Lef.
fulvifrons Jac. n. sp.

Demotina.
serraticollis Baly.
*sumatrana Jac.

Trichochrysea.
evanescens Baly.
hirta Fab.

Cleorina.
*aulica Lef.
fulvitarsis Lef.
malayana Jac.
nigrita Jac.
*ornata Jac.

Pyropida
sumptuosa Baly.

Rhyparida.
pinguis Baly.

Abirus.
piceipes Baly.

Corynodes.
fraternus Baly.

Colasposoma.
splendidum Fab.
inconstans Baly.
mutabile Baly.
nigriventre Baly.

Colaspoides.
fulvitarsis Jac. n. sp.
Modiglianii Jac.
nigripes Jac.

Chrysomelinae.

Agasta.
formosa Hope.

Chalcolampra.
octodecimguttata Fab.

Halticinae.

Acrocrypta.
dimidiata Baly.

Duvivieri Jac. n. sp.
gibbosa Jac. n. sp.
Mouhoti Baly.

Nisotra.
gemella Erichs.

Haltica.
cyanea Web.
birmanensis Jac.

Lactica.
sumatrana Jac.

Aphthona.
sumatrana Jac.

Phyllotreta.
Downesi Baly.

Sphaerometopa.
acroleuca Wied.
*imitans Jac.
obsoleta Jac.

Chaloenus.
abdominalis Jac. n. sp.
*capitatus Jac.
latifrons Westw.
subcostatus Jac. n. sp.

Hyphasis.
abdominalis Jac. n. sp.
biplagiata Jac. n. sp.
inconstans Jac.
parvula Jac.
unifasciata Jac.

Cerotrus.
bimaculatus Jac.

Docemasia.
caerulea Jac. n. sp.

Sebaethe.
affinis Jac.

depressa Jac. n. sp.
fusca Fab.
sumatrana Jac.

Argopus.
angulicollis Clark.

Sphaeroderma.
cyanipennis Jac.
*flavoplagiata Jac.
*limbatipennis Jac.
*Modiglianii Jac.
*nigromarginata Jac.
parvula Jac.
semiregularis Jac. n. sp.
seminigra Jac. n. sp.
striatipennis Jac.
*sumatrana Jac.
varipennis Jac.

Eucycla.
*elegantula Jac.

Ophrida.
nigripennis Baly.

Psylliodes
Balyi Jac.
*fulvipes Jac.

Allomorpha.
*glabrata Jac.

Euneamera.
sumatrensis Har.

Gallerucidae.

Oides.
apicalis Jac.
duodecimpunctata Clark.
metallica Jac.
pectoralis Clark.
sumatrensis Blanch.

Aulacophora.
antennata Baly.
apicipes Jac.
atripennis Fabr.
Batesi Jac.
bicolor Web.
Boisduvali Baly.
coffeae Horn.
cornuta Baly.
denticornis Jac.
Dohrni Jac. n. sp.
flavomarginata Duviv.
frontalis Baly.
luteicornis Fab.
orientalis Horn.
palliata Fab.
postica Chap.
quadrimaculata Chap.
rosea Fab.
*similis Oliv.
terminata Jac. n. sp.

Pseudocophora.
brunnea Baly.
Erichsoni Baly.
*sumatrana Jac.

Phyllobrotica.
unicolor Illig.

Malacosoma.
cyanicollis Jac.
viridis Jac.

Miltina.
dilatata Chap.

Ozomena.
Dohrni Jac. n. sp.

impressa Fab.
intermedia Jac. n. sp.
nigricollis Jac.

Mimastra.
fulvipennis Jac.
pallida Jac.
Platteeuwi Duviv.
rugosa Jac.
violaceipennis Jac.

Xenoda.
*basalis Jac.
parvula Jac. n. sp.
spinicornis Baly.

Sastra.
apicicornis Jac. n. sp.
*sulcicollis Jac.

Sastroides.
bimaculatus Jac.
crassipalpis Jac. n. sp.
fuscipennis Jac. n. sp.
unicolor Jac.

Emathea.
aeneipennis Baly.
*Balyi Jac.
*fulvicornis Jac.
intermedia Jac. n. sp.
violaceipennis Baly.

Cynorta.
capitata Jac.
pallipes Jac. n. sp.
variabilis Jac.

Diorhabda.
robusta Jac. n. sp.

Gallerucella.
Hageni Jac.

multimaculata Jac.
rugosa Jac.
Sastracella.
sumatrana Jac. n. sp.
Orthoxia.
Boisduvali Clark.
Cerophysa.
nodicornis Wied
sumatrensis Jac.
viridipennis Jac.
Nadrana.
bella Baly.
pallidicornis Baly.
Raapi Jac.
Arcastes.
biplagiatus Baly.
sanguineus Jac.
suturalis Jac.
Haplosoma.
abdominalis Jac.
Haplosomoides.
serena Boh.
Sumatrasia.
unicolor Jac.
Niasia.
caeruleipennis Jac.
Eustheta.
variabilis Jac.
Metellus.
fulvicollis Jac.
laevipennis Jac.
nigripennis Jac. n. sp.
Dorydea.
insignis Baly.
*nigripennis Jac.

Platyxantha.
apicalis Baly.
apicicornis Jac.
bifasciata Jac. n. sp.
coxalis Jac. n. sp.
monstrosa Jac. n. sp.
nigrolimbata Jac. n. sp.
sumatrana Jac. n. sp.
Aenidea.
Jacobyi Baly.
laeta Baly.
pallipes Fab.
sumatrensis Jac.
Paridea.
diversa Jac.
livida Duviv.
Haplosonyx.
albicornis Wied.
batuensis Jac.
*basalis Jac.
nigricollis Duviv.
pallidus Jac.
parvulus Jac.
Sumatrae Web.
Caritheca.
quadripustulata Baly.
Goniopleura.
bicoloripes Gah.
Sermyloides.
basalis Jac.
Syoplia.
javanensis Jac.
Monolepta.
*approximans Jac.
basalis Jac.

basimarginata Boisd.
brunneipennis Jac.
elegantula Boh.
*nigromarginata Jac.
quadrinotata Fab.
rufipennis Jac. n. sp.
terminata Guér.

Eumelepta.
biplagiata Jac.

Ochralea.
flava Oliv.
marginata Jac.
pectoralis Har.

Candezea.
C-album Jac. n. sp.
circumducta Jac. n. sp.
discoidalis Jac.
*impressicollis Jac.
laticornis Jac. n. sp.
nigrilabrum Jac. n. sp.

Neolepta.
biplagiata Jac.

Microlepta.
pallida Jac.

Coeligethes.
submetallica Jac.
unicolor Jac.

Antipha.
abdominalis Jac.
Feae Jac.
fulvofrontalis Jac.
nigra Jac.
*similis Jac.
*tenuimarginata Jac.
*variabilis Jac.
Wallacei Jac. n. sp.

Macrima.
flavoplagiata Jac. n. sp.
fuscolineata Jac.
nigromarginata Jac. n. sp.
subcostata Jac.

Solenia.
robusta Jac.

Euphymasia.
Dohrni Jac. n. sp.

Pseudeustheta.
quadriplagiata Jac. n. sp.

Stethidea.
Balyi Duviv.

Homelea.
variabilis Jac.

www.ingramcontent.com/pod-product-compliance
Lightning Source LLC
Chambersburg PA
CBHW021631270326
41931CB00008B/972

* 9 7 8 3 7 4 1 1 3 0 5 3 3 *